GATEWAY FRAMEWORK

A GOVERNANCE APPROACH FOR INFRASTRUCTURE INVESTMENT SUSTAINABILITY

JUNE 2023

ASIAN DEVELOPMENT BANK

ADB

© 2023 Asian Development Bank
6 ADB Avenue, Mandaluyong City, 1550 Metro Manila, Philippines
Tel +63 2 8632 4444; Fax +63 2 8636 2444
www.adb.org

Some rights reserved. Published in 2023.

ISBN 978-92-9270-180-2 (print); 978-92-9270-181-9 (electronic); 978-92-9270-182-6 (ebook)
Publication Stock No. TCS230225
DOI: http://dx.doi.org/10.22617/TCS230225

Note:
In this publication, "$" refers to United States dollars and "A$" refers to Australian dollars.

Cover design by Maro de Guzman.

Contents

Tables, Figures, and Boxes

Foreword

Global challenges such as climate change and the fiscal costs of transitioning to a net-zero economy, gender, and digitization impose greater complexity in the choice and design of infrastructure projects. The Asian Development Bank (ADB) is engaging clients more deeply, not just on leveraging and mobilizing private capital to meet these challenges, but also providing knowledge solutions such as this report on the Gateway Process to ensure that governments maximize the efficiency of infrastructure investment at a time of scarce public resources, and that projects are well planned and deliver value for money.

Governments require strong institutions and capacities to manage finite resources and maximize the economic potential of infrastructure investments to deliver equitable access to affordable services. This publication contributes to the work of ministries of finance, planning, budget, and related agencies by helping governments to establish a Gateway Process for the preparation and procurement of public–private partnership (PPP) and traditional public investment projects. The Gateway Process analyzes projects at the main decision points over the entire project cycle and prevents projects from going forward during the project preparation cycle if it deems the project to be economically unviable, inefficient as a PPP, or fiscally unaffordable. Beyond fiscal issues, the Gateway Process helps to ensure strategic fit with national priorities; contributes to transparency and accountability; ensures a more rigorous review process including for climate and environmental, social, and governance issues; and builds confidence in the integrity of the project. If modifications are necessary, the Gateway Process can stop project authorities from compounding design deficiencies before they can negatively impact a project.

This publication builds on prior ADB knowledge products aimed at helping policy makers in developing countries improve institutional capacity for quality infrastructure investment and fiscal management. These publications include *An Infrastructure Governance Approach to Fiscal Management in State-Owned Enterprises and Public–Private Partnerships*, which explains how quality infrastructure investment can address issues around tight fiscal spaces and rising debt, and help maximize economic benefits at the lowest cost. ADB's *Supporting Quality Infrastructure in Developing Asia* identifies weak public investment management capacity as a limitation to reduce the infrastructure gap and highlights the importance of investment efficiency, life-cycle costs, disaster resilience, and infrastructure governance.

When it comes to strengthening public investment management, no single solution fits all economies and institutions. The Gateway Process does, however, provide a framework that can be applied to fit the needs of individual countries and institutional capacity. Policy makers can use this framework to determine how best to develop their own Gateway Process within their wider policies and processes for public investment management.

Acknowledgments

This report is led by Hanif Rahemtulla, principal public management specialist, Governance Thematic Group of the Sustainable Development and Climate Change Department (SDTC-GOV); Michael Schur, infrastructure finance specialist; and David Bloomgarden, public investment management specialist. We acknowledge the helpful comments provided by Hiranya Mukhopadhyay, chief, SDTC-GOV; and Isabelle Chauche, senior PPP specialist, Office of Public–Private Partnership.

Abbreviations

ADB	Asian Development Bank
CCEA	Cabinet Committee on Economic Affairs
COVID-19	coronavirus disease
DMC	developing member country
GCAs	Gateway Coordination Agencies
GDP	gross domestic product
IIGF	Indonesia Infrastructure Guarantee Fund
NSW	New South Wales
PFM	public financial management
PIM	public investment management
PIMA	Public Investment Management Assessment
PPP	public–private partnership
SOE	state-owned enterprise
UK	United Kingdom

About the Authors

Michael Schur, Infrastructure Finance Specialist

Schur has over 25 years of global experience as an infrastructure finance and investment specialist, and has chief executive experience in both the public and private sectors. He is currently an independent board member of a private concessions investment company and advisor to private and public sector clients, both in Australia and internationally. He has conducted risk assessments, project structuring, financial due diligence, and commercial negotiations on over 25 privately financed infrastructure projects with a combined value in excess of $30 billion in countries including Australia, Cambodia, Ethiopia, India, Indonesia, New Zealand, the Philippines, South Africa, Uganda, and Viet Nam. He has a particular interest in infrastructure governance and in designing fiscal frameworks for managing infrastructure programs, whether delivered via public–private partnerships (PPPs) or by state-owned corporations.

David Bloomgarden, PPP and Public Investment Management Consultant

With over 3 decades of experience in policy, management, and project design and implementation, Bloomgarden is an expert in public investment and PPPs. During his tenure as the chief of the Inclusive City Unit at the Inter-American Development Bank (IADB), he managed a $44.5-million project in Latin America and the Caribbean region, overseeing the development of 40 blended finance investments for small and medium-sized enterprises in sustainable business models for urban services delivery. As the lead private sector specialist for PPPs, Bloomgarden spearheaded the IADB's Program to Promote PPPs in Latin America and the Caribbean, providing technical assistance to governments to enhance policy, project preparation, and implementation for sustainable infrastructure. He also created a PPP Readiness Index called "Infrascope," which was published by the Economist Intelligence Unit and used to assess PPP institutional capacity in Latin America and the Caribbean. After departing from the IADB, he has worked as a PPP consultant for organizations such as the World Bank (Global Infrastructure Facility), the Asian Development Bank, and the European Bank for Reconstruction and Development, offering counsel on public investment management and quality infrastructure investment.

1 Introduction

Rapid urbanization in Asia in recent decades has had a palpable impact on the infrastructure gap plaguing the region, where the lack of access to quality basic services in water, power, and transportation is occurring in many developing countries despite the region's significant technological and economic gains. As a response to the growing need to improve access to sustainable infrastructure and infrastructure services, the Asian Development Bank (ADB), in line with the ADB Strategy 2030 operational priority of strengthening governance and institutional capacity, has developed technical assistance projects and lending operations that strengthen public sector capacity to prepare and implement infrastructure investments—including through public–private partnerships (PPPs)—that are fiscally sustainable and achieve their development objectives.[1] ADB support for infrastructure governance is in line with QII Principles for Promoting Quality Infrastructure Investment, which were presented at the G7 Ise-Shima Summit in 2016 and supported by G20 Leaders at the Osaka Summit in 2019.[2] The principles cite value for money and fiscal sustainability, governance to ensure transparency and integrity, sound regulatory and legal framework, as well as climate resiliency, gender, and environmental and social safeguards. These principles aim to maximize the social, environmental, and economic impact of infrastructure.[3]

In addition to the challenge of rapid urbanization in the Asia and Pacific region, some ADB developing member countries (DMCs) had very high debt levels prior to the coronavirus disease (COVID-19) pandemic. DMCs are facing considerable fiscal challenges and high levels of debt due to the urgent need to deal with the economic and health consequences of COVID-19. Further, DMCs face these challenges within the wider context of the imperative to finance climate disaster resilience, climate-proofing planned public investments, mitigating emissions in line with Nationally Determined Contributions under the Paris Accords, and undertaking adaptation to reduce the economic and social losses of climate change. To help overcome fiscal and debt challenges, governments will need to crowd in private sector investment, including using capital market mechanisms such as de-risking funds created by various countries and ADB to create bankable, affordable, and sustainable infrastructure projects. One example of such a mechanism is the ASEAN Catalytic Green Finance Facility. This facility, launched in 2019, uses a de-risking approach to bridge funding gaps and develop bankable green investment projects in infrastructure that mobilize private investment, know-how, and technology. It has the capacity to use sovereign guarantees and blended finance to de-risk projects during the riskiest period of project development, which is the construction and early operational stages.[4]

By improving public investment management (PIM), DMCs can prioritize the implementation of projects that are most effective, affordable, and sustainable—and provide the best value for money within current and future budgetary constraints and reassuring the market on their ability to undertake long-term commitments. PIM is a comprehensive framework for infrastructure governance across the three key stages of the public investment cycle: (i) investment planning, (ii) allocation of investment based on project

---

1. Some examples include ADB regional technical assistance on Strengthening Fiscal Governance and Sustainability in Public–Private Partnerships and on Improving Infrastructure and State-Owned Enterprise Governance for Sustainable Investment and Debt Management.
2. ADB. 2021. *Supporting Quality Infrastructure in Developing Asia*. Manila. This report analyzes the importance of quality infrastructure governance, focusing on the impact of weak public investment management capacity as a constraint to allocating public resources effectively to maximize the economic benefits from infrastructure investment. It is aligned with the G20 Principles for Quality Infrastructure Investment to increase economic efficiency, ensure funding of life-cycle costs, build resilience against disasters, enhance infrastructure governance, and ensure sustainable public finances.
3. G20 Leaders Communique. September 2016, Hangzhou.
4. ADB. 2020. *Green Finance Strategies for Post-COVID-19 Economic Recovery in Southeast Asia: Greening Recoveries for Planet and People*. Manila.

evaluation, and (iii) implementation of priority projects. A key part of this is governance surrounding project progression through the various development stages, ensuring that the right approval steps are inserted into the process to determine when projects should progress through each stage of development and that the right expertise is available to decision makers at each approval step. PIM also includes ongoing project monitoring during the operational phase, and independent audit of projects, typically by national audit offices, and legislative branch oversight of public investment. Improving PIM is essential for DMCs to create and accelerate green recoveries given the substantial accumulated fiscal constraints.

The Gateway Process, first developed in the early 2000s by the Office of Government Commerce of the United Kingdom (UK), mandates independent reviews of projects at prescribed stages of the project life cycle. Evidence from the UK shows that based on value-for-money reviews, the average cost avoidance is between 3% and 5% when best practices for Gateway Process reviews are implemented from the earliest stages of the project cycle. For example, an average Gateway Process costs $10,000 to review a $100-million project but could generate average costs savings of between $3 million and $5 million.[5] The primary aim is to ensure that the project's stated benefits and objectives are likely to be achieved on time and on budget. It does this by clarifying objectives and success criteria for the project with the project team, ensuring that robust planning has been carried out up front, and by assessing if all key project risks have been identified and mitigated as far as possible. The Gateway Process review team typically makes recommendations where gaps in any of these areas have been discovered through the review. A Gateway Process has the potential to provide a governance framework to help DMCs bring forward for funding and financing solely those infrastructure projects that are not only effective and fiscally affordable but achieve climate benefits and deliver value for money. By doing so, DMCs can ensure the allocation of scarce public resources to the best projects in line with government priorities, reduce unanticipated fiscal consequences such as cost overruns or project delays, and support public investment efficiency and fiscal sustainability. The UK Gateway Process requires a sequence of reviews by a panel of independent experts at each phase of the project cycle. The panel reviews the objectives of the project, identifies and resolves issues or errors in project development at each phase of the project cycle, reviews the planning process, and confirms that a project will likely achieve its benefits and objectives. Box 1 shows the key phases in the UK process to review infrastructure projects.

Box 1: Key Phases in the United Kingdom Gateway Process Reviews

Strategic Assessment—reviews program objectives and linkage to the ministry strategy.

Business Justification—confirms that the project is in line with business needs and is likely to deliver value for money.

Delivery Strategy—analysis of assumptions and proposed approach within the delivery strategy to ensure suitability.

Investment Decision—analysis of governance arrangements and the business case for the investment to ensure the project will deliver value for money.

Readiness for Service—assesses readiness to move from planning to implementation and the capacity of service providers and delivery partners.

Operations Review and Benefits Realization—investigate if benefits identified in the business case are realized, and if there are any issues that would impact implementation of operations.

Source: Global Infrastructure Hub. Gateway Review Process. https://www.gihub.org/resources/publications/gateway-review-process.

---

[5]   J. Wanna, ed. 2007. *Improving Implementation: Organisational Change and Project Management.* Chapter 17. ANU Press. See also UK Infrastructure and Projects Authority. 2019. *Gateway Review Process Review: Report of Findings and Recommendations.*

Research has shown that both institutional design, i.e., the organizational structure, rules, procedures, and policies on paper, and the effectiveness by which institutions achieve their intended purpose, matter for the quality of country overall PIM frameworks. Public investment and fiscal management policies thus need effective institutions to ensure the implementation of such policies in a consistent and fiscally sustainable manner. The value addition of this technical note is to provide relevant information to practitioners and policy makers wishing to adapt or improve upon a Gateway Process and integrate this within their own PIM governance frameworks.[6] In the following sections, this paper describes the current fiscal context within which DMCs are operating and the need for more efficient public investment (Section 2); sets out the key principles and elements of the Governance Gateway model and its role in improving PIM, and surveys how Gateway models have been deployed in a range of country contexts including DMCs (Section 3); provides recommendations for how DMCs can incorporate the Gateway Process model into their own PIM processes (Section 4); and the conclusion highlights the links between Gateway processes and broader governance approaches for infrastructure investment sustainability (Section 5).

---

[6]   PIM, as used in this paper, refers to the regulatory and oversight system used to plan, allocate investments, and implement sustainable and resilient public investments. It is a subcomponent of public financial management (PFM). The term "public financial management" commonly refers to the annual budget cycle, including (i) budget formulation, (ii) budget execution and procurement, (iii) accounting and reporting, and (iv) external security and audit.

2 Current Asian Context and Need for More Efficient Public Investment

Asia's public infrastructure investment faces a perfect storm of preexisting infrastructure gaps, lower revenue, and higher debt levels following the COVID-19 economic contraction, compounded by the wide-ranging impacts of the Russian invasion of Ukraine and the imperative of responding to climate change. Even before the challenges of recent years, substantial infrastructure gaps existed throughout Asia. The COVID-19 pandemic introduced immense fiscal pressures. Asian countries have been forced to spend trillions of dollars on controlling the virus, protecting people, and propping up the economy. Beyond additional expenditure, fiscal revenues have fallen due to the immediate and ongoing economic contractions that the pandemic has caused.

ADB's *Asian Development Outlook* lowered the projection of economic growth for developing Asia from 5.2% to 4.3% for 2022, and from 5.3% to 4.9% for 2023.[7] For a global economy that is already struggling to deal with the aftereffects of the pandemic, the ongoing Russian invasion of Ukraine has produced alarming cascading effects with particularly massive impacts on developing countries. Ukraine and the Russian Federation are major commodity producers, accounting for about 30% of the global exports for wheat and barley. In addition, the Russian Federation is the largest natural gas exporter and the second largest crude oil exporter in the world. All countries have been affected, including through disruptions in global supply chains, sharp rises in inflation, volatility in capital flows, and hardening of interest rates. Among ADB DMCs, the largest impacts are likely to be in Central and West Asian countries that have relatively strong economic relations with the Russian Federation and Ukraine. In the short and medium term, these countries are expected to be impacted via reductions in foreign direct and institutional investment, trade, remittances, and tourism. These events will impact countries with high debt levels. However, not all DMCs are in the same position—while some countries have high debt levels, others have moderate and low debt levels. However, those countries with high and moderate debt levels are considered to have no or very limited fiscal capacity—either to bridge the infrastructure gap and/or to invest in climate change mitigation or adaptation.[8]

The deceleration in economic growth and inflationary trends will make it harder to finance and fund low-carbon and climate-resilient investments. Climate change is one of the biggest challenges confronting policy makers worldwide. The long-term growth potential, livelihoods, and well-being of all countries in the Asia and Pacific region are at risk due to climate change. The region is experiencing faster temperature increases compared to most other areas, and is already the most vulnerable to weather-related disasters such as hurricanes, droughts, and wildfires, which are projected to intensify in frequency and severity. Moreover, rising sea levels pose a direct threat to about a billion people in the region by 2050, potentially submerging several megacities and posing existential threats to some Pacific island countries.[9]

While the nature of the localized impacts of climate change for each DMC differs, all must implement adaptation measures to increase their resilience and reduce physical and economic damage. Investment in adaptation adds another fiscal pressure on top of those already described. The impact of climate change varies and, therefore, adaptation costs will also vary. In Figure 1, the purple bars represent Pacific countries, and

---

[7]   ADB. 2022. *Asian Development Outlook 2022 Update: Entrepreneurship in the Digital Age.* Manila.

[8]   ADB. 2022. *The Sustainability of Asia's Debt: Problems, Policies, and Practices.* Manila.

[9]   ADB. 2017. *Climate Change Operational Framework 2017–2030 Enhanced Actions to Low Greenhouse Gas Emission and Climate-Resilient Development.* Manila.

the orange bars represent the rest of Asia and Pacific countries. The bars represent public sector retrofitting costs and coastal protection costs as a percentage of gross domestic product (GDP). The level of protection calculated corresponds to the protection level that keeps average annual losses to below 0.01% of GDP for protected areas. The Pacific Island countries face the highest costs of adaptation due to their smaller economies and high vulnerability to the impacts of climate change. Strengthening adaptive capacity for the Asia and Pacific region overall will require higher annual public investment spending of approximately 3.3% of GDP.[10] It is possible that some investment projects can be easily made climate resilient through upgrades, which would be relatively inexpensive. However, for other projects that involve existing critical assets exposed to climate risks, more extensive measures may be necessary, such as reinforcing stormwater systems and constructing coastal protection infrastructure, which can be considerably more expensive. In countries with limited fiscal space, financing options for these additional investments include exploring greater domestic revenue mobilization, which is feasible in the region, and improving the prioritization and efficiency of public investment spending.[11]

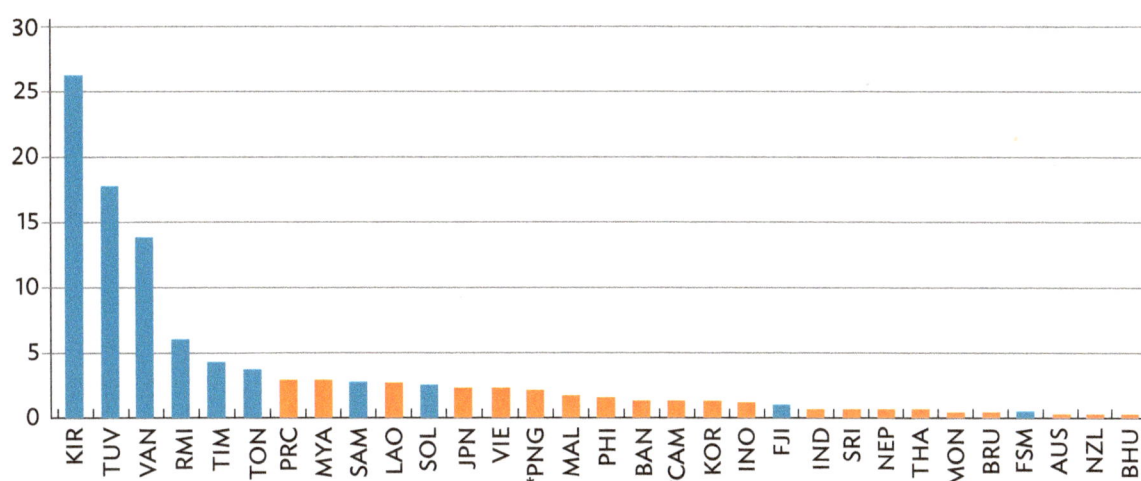

Figure 1: Public Annual Adaptation Costs
(% of GDP)

AUS = Australia, BAN = Bangladesh, BHU = Bhutan, BRU = Brunei Darussalam, CAM = Cambodia, FIJ = Fiji, FSM = Federated States of Micronesia, GDP = gross domestic product, IND = India, INO = Indonesia, JPN = Japan, KIR = Kiribati, KOR = Republic of Korea, LAO =Lao People's Democratic Republic, MAL = Malaysia, MON = Mongolia, MYA = Myanmar, NEP = Nepal, NZL = New Zealand, PHI = Philippines, PNG = Papua New Guinea, PRC = People's Republic of China, RMI = Marshall Islands, SAM = Samoa, SOL = Solomon Islands, SRI = Sri Lanka, THA = Thailand, TIM = Timor-Leste, TON = Tonga, TUV = Tuvalu, VAN = Vanuatu, VIE = Viet Nam.

Note: The blue bars represent Pacific island countries, and the orange bars represent all other Asia–Pacific countries. Bars correspond to the sum of upgrading and retrofitting costs in the public sector and coastal protection cost. The level of protection being costed corresponds to the protection that keeps average annual losses below 0.01% of local GDP to protected areas. Data labels in the figure use International Organization for Standardization (ISO) country codes.

* Missing values in the risk Intolerance case for Cambodia and for the private sector for Papua New Guinea.

Source: E. Dabla-Norris et al. 2021. Fiscal Policies to Address Climate Change in Asia and the Pacific. {IMF Departmental Paper}. No 2021/007. 24 March. IMF.

---

[10]   E. Dabla-Norris et al. 2021. Fiscal Policies to Address Climate Change in Asia and the Pacific. *IMF Departmental Paper*. No 2021/007. 24 March. IMF.
[11]   E. Go et al. 2022. Developing Asia's Fiscal Landscape and Challenges. *ADB Economics Working Paper Series*. No. 665. Manila: ADB. This paper shows tax revenues in developing Asia tended to rise from 2000 onward, but continued to lag high-income economies and some developing peers. COVID-19 fiscal measures, combined with the downturn in revenues, have significantly weakened public finances in many DMCs.

A. Options for Improving Fiscal Space and Debt Sustainability

Although ADB's recent analysis suggests current debt levels are sustainable for many countries, fiscal headroom is limited, so DMCs should utilize available levers to position themselves for a green-led economic recovery—including increasing revenues and increasing public investment in infrastructure as well as rightsizing expenditures. Such green-led recoveries would be required to respond to climate change as well as make progress toward achieving the Sustainable Development Goals. The relative mix of these levers utilized in each DMC will depend on its unique characteristics—particularly given the potential for economic efficiency from optimizing tax expenditures—forgone taxes—and greater efficiency in the collection of value-added taxes, including taxes on the growing digital economy.[12] ADB's recent update to Asian Development Outlook 2022 explicitly considers opportunities for increasing revenues, suggesting that "significant opportunities exist to expand the use of tax and other fiscal instruments to tackle environmental and health priorities while raising revenue. Fundamental tax reform to mobilize revenue better can be achieved and it is best done in tandem with efforts to strengthen tax administration and improve taxpayer morale." The update suggests that there is potential across the region to improve collection of tax revenue from the pre-pandemic average of approximately 16%of GDP by around 3 to 4 percentage points. Comparisons between ADB DMCs is shown in Figure 2.

Figure 2: Average Tax Revenue in Selected Asian Economies, 2000–2004 versus 2015–2019
(% of GDP)

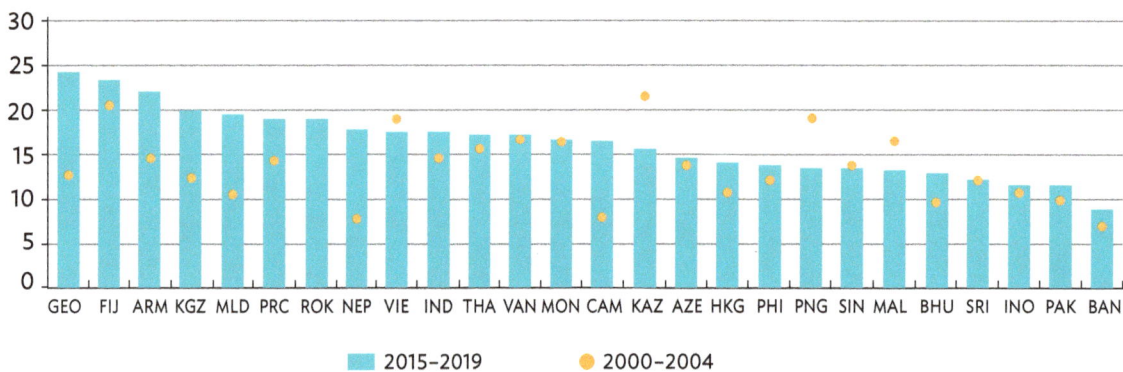

ARM = Armenia; AZE = Azerbaijan; BAN = Bangladesh; BHU = Bhutan; CAM = Cambodia; FIJ = Fiji; GDP = gross domestic product; GEO = Georgia; HKG = Hong Kong, China; IND = India; INO = Indonesia; KAZ = Kazakhstan; KGZ = Kyrgyz Republic; MAL = Malaysia; MLD = Maldives; MON = Mongolia, NEP = Nepal; PAK = Pakistan; PHI = Philippines; PNG = Papua New Guinea; PRC = People's Republic of China; ROK = Republic of Korea, SIN = Singapore; SRI = Sri Lanka; THA = Thailand; VAN = Vanuatu; VIE = Viet Nam.

Note: See Go et al. (2022) for details.

Sources: OECD. *Global Revenue Statistics Database; International Monetary Fund. Government Finance Statistics online database* (both accessed 31 January 2022); and ADB estimates.

Increasing public investment in infrastructure will need to be a vital component of the post-COVID-19 recovery. This is because there is compelling evidence that efficient and productive infrastructure investment will, in the medium to long term, not only raise GDP but will cause debt-to-GDP ratios to fall and maximize the economic and fiscal gains in a fiscally constrained environment. For decision makers to ensure fiscal sustainability, facilitate GDP growth, and lower debt-to-GDP levels, it is critically important that such investment is of the highest possible quality, i.e., the right infrastructure delivering maximum economic benefits at the lowest cost.

Efficient public investment can raise both short- and long-term outputs, stimulate private investment, and is essential to grapple with limited fiscal space and increasing debt resulting from the fiscal pressures. Several studies confirm the positive relationship between levels of GDP and gross fixed capital formation, and that the economic impact of public investment is higher than all other forms of public spending, especially in the medium term.[13] However, the economic benefits of public investment in infrastructure are not guaranteed— increasing investment quality (i.e., efficiency and productivity) is critical for mitigating the possible trade-off between higher output and higher public debt-to-GDP ratios. Countries with a high degree of public investment efficiency achieve almost four times the positive multiplier effects than other countries—both in the short and medium term.[14]

B. Measuring the Current Performance Gap in Developing Member Country Public Infrastructure Investment

While domestic resource mobilization needs to be part of the mix, decision makers should give priority to maximizing the investment in public infrastructure, in particular investment that enables both mitigation and adaptation to climate risk. Given limited fiscal space, it will be essential that Asian countries maximize efficiency with respect to their public investments. The IMF has attempted to measure PIM performance by means of a Public Investment Efficiency Index, which estimates the relationship between a country's public capital stock and indicators of access and the quality of infrastructure assets.[15] Applying the index to over 100 countries, the IMF found that the average efficiency gap for the Asia and Pacific region is 32%, defined as the gap assessed against the top-performing countries by region.

Closing the efficiency gap requires strengthening PIM governance arrangements across the three key PIM stages: planning, allocation, and implementation. Governance arrangements in each stage depend, in turn, on the strength in both design and effectiveness of key PIM "institution"(Figures 3). The former identifies relevant PIM institutions in planning (1–5), allocation (6–10), and implementation (11–15), noting scores by income level based on the Public Investment Management Assessment (PIMA) undertaken by the IMF in various countries between 2015 and 2019, including 11 countries in Asia and Pacific. The PIMA measures institutional design and effectiveness on a scale of 1 to 3, with best practice being a score of 3. The analysis suggests that all countries, including emerging markets and low-income developing countries, have significant scope to improve infrastructure governance and increase the effectiveness of public investment. What emerges is that governance institutions are strongest in the early phase of the investment cycle (e.g., when establishing fiscal targets and

---

[13]   A. Abiad, D. Furceri, and P. Topalova. 2015. The Macroeconomic Effects of Public Investment: Evidence from Advanced Economies. *IMF Working Paper*; Global Infrastructure Hub (GIH) Preliminary findings on quantifying the economic impact of infrastructure investment, Third G20 Infrastructure Working Group: Virtual Meeting 9 June 2020. PRELIMINARY FINDINGS. GIH analyzed over 3,000 estimates of the fiscal multiplier—a ratio of the increase in GDP after 1 year (impact multiplier) and at 2–5 years (cumulative multiplier) that results from an increase in public spending—from over 200 academic papers from the last 25 years. GIH also analyzed over 600 estimates of the effect of public investment on long-run productivity, from 170 academic papers.

[14]   A. Abiad, D. Furceri, and P. Topalova. 2015. The Macroeconomic Effects of Public Investment: Evidence from Advanced Economies. *IMF Working Paper*.

[15]   IMF. 2015. *Making Public Investment More Efficient*.

rules, formulation of national and sector plans), but considerably weaker when these PIM frameworks and rules need to be converted into effective allocation of resources and implementation of projects, mainly due to capacity constraints in project selection, inadequate spending on maintenance, and poor asset management. Figure 3 shows the scores on a scale of 1 to 3 for institutional design versus effectiveness. Institutional design measures whether the governance institution exists, whereas institutional effectiveness is a measure of its relative effectiveness (i.e., what is on paper versus what is in practice). The Asia and Pacific region tends to be stronger in the areas of institutional design than institutional effectiveness.

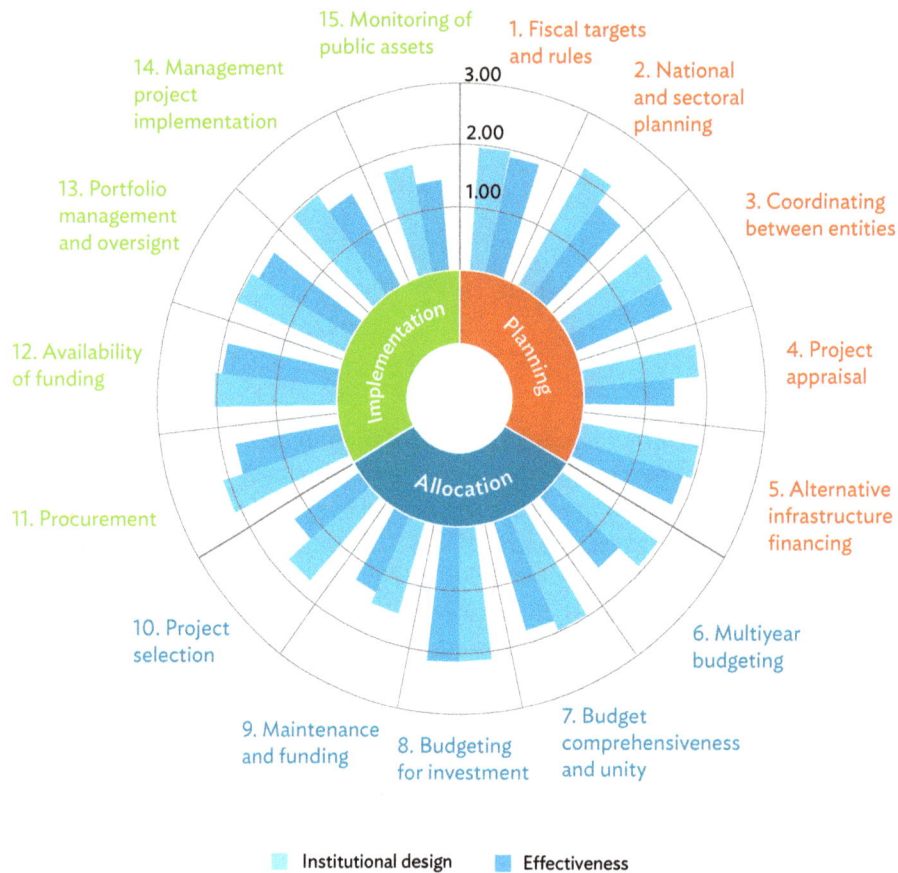

Figure 3: Asia and Pacific Region—Institutional Design versus Effectiveness

Note: The further away fom the center, the higher the public investment management assessment (PIMA) score.

Source: International Monetary Fund. Infrastructure Governance Website PIMA Regional Data (accessed 1 February 2023).

C. The Need for "Greening" Public Investment Management Processes

In addition to the general challenges of implementing PIM well, DMCs will also now need to do so in ways that respond to the need for climate change mitigation and adaptation.[16] Strong and effective PIM institutions and capacity will help countries carry out public investments efficiently and enable the public investment budget to go further. This applies to both traditional public investment and for PPPs. As is the case for all public policy, institutional, and governance reforms, prioritization and trade-offs will be necessary to find the best balance among social and economic, environmental, and the costs and benefits of specific reforms to improve public investment. A Gateway Process is linked to the quality of the PIM framework and, at a broader level, the quality of public financial management. Reforms should be individually tailored to the strengths and weaknesses of these governance frameworks. Several assessment frameworks help identify aspects of the PIM framework, including for climate, and help to prioritize reforms.[17] While no one governance solution applies to all economies, there are five overall priority areas for the integration of climate considerations into the PIM cycle—in procedures, policies, or methodologies:

(i) **Planning:** It is essential to align national and sector plans and associated investment portfolios with climate objectives to transform public sector infrastructure toward climate resilience and sustainability. The planning phase is particularly relevant for incorporating climate considerations into spatial planning and construction requirements.

(ii) **Coordination:** Public investment involves various layers of government, state-owned enterprises (SOEs), and PPPs. Thus, integrating green considerations into public investment management requires coordination across all parts of the public sector, including joint ventures with the private sector.

(iii) **Appraisal and selection:** The decision-making process for major infrastructure projects relies on crucial phases of appraisal and selection. These phases determine which projects will be implemented, making it essential to include climate-related analysis of mitigation and adaptation impacts in the decision-making process.

(iv) **Budget and portfolio management:** Budget allocations for green investments and maintenance should be included in annual budgets and other fiscal instruments such as the medium-term expenditure framework and government financial statements. Asset management, ex post audit, and review should similarly consider climate objectives.

(v) **Fiscal risk management:** Climate change risks potentially impact public infrastructure and budgets. Incorporating climate considerations in disaster management strategies and fiscal risk analyses is important, and risk mitigation strategies should also consider climate-related risks.

---

[16] See, for example, IMF. 2021. Strengthening Infrastructure Governance for Climate-Responsive Public Investment. *Policy Paper.* No. 2021/076.

[17] ADB. 2022. Green Public Investment Management of Infrastructure: Governance Aspects of Strengthening Infrastructure Sustainability. *ADB Governance Brief.* This paper identifies diagnostic instruments to assess and prioritize reforms. These diagnostics include IMF: Public Investment Management Assessment (PIMA) and Climate Module (C-PIMA); UNDP: Climate Public Expenditure and Institutional Review (CPEIR); PEFA Partners: Public Expenditure and Financial Accountability (PEFA) and Climate Diagnostic (Climate PEFA); World Bank: Diagnostic and Infrastructure Governance (InfraGov).

3 Gateway Processes—Key Elements and Applications

Gateway Processes strengthen the scrutiny applied at approval steps within the PIM process. It is a valuable method of further increasing PIM performance and reducing the infrastructure performance gap in DMCs. The Gateway Process is a series of decision points where the Ministry of Finance or similar agency approval is necessary at each major step of the preparation and implementation parts of the cycle. It provides a space for a sequential review of decisions and allows the finance ministry or similarly constituted agency to prevent early on projects that do not provide evidence of value for money, including fiscal sustainability, from moving forward. Experience shows that such Gateway Process is a much superior solution to the often-unrealistic gatekeeper role given to and expected from finance ministries.

Deciding which projects to do and how to do them involves answering many questions. Is the project financially viable? Is the project resilient to climate change? Which project is the best one to achieve the required service-level increase? Answering these many questions involves undertaking analysis in a sequential manner over the project cycle. For example, investment planning and project selection must occur before project-level appraisal can be undertaken to avoid overinvesting scarce public resources; in analysis, that may turn out to be unnecessary and allow projects to "fail fast." The sequential approach enables decision makers to prioritize projects as a first step. Doing full and costly project appraisals on all projects before prioritizing them would waste scarce resources on projects that may not be selected at all or will be undertaken later. Equally, determining the optimal procurement method for a project (the "procurement decision") should only occur once the project is determined to be economically viable (the "investment decision"). Each of these stages creates a natural step at which projects undergo assessment to determine whether the project should progress to the next stage of development.

A Gateway Process can help offset undue political or vested interest influence on the process of selecting and approving projects. At a minimum, an effective Gateway Process can help avoid "white elephant" projects. Vested interest seeking to accelerate approval of a project may exert pressure on agencies to overlook unfavorable technical analysis. Having strong policies, guidelines, or legislative backing for a Gateway Process can help manage vested interests, including from private lobbyists and contractors, that may weaken the project stages of planning and preparing, funding, and ensuring fiscal sustainability.[18]

The Gateway Process achieves additional scrutiny by requiring independent peer review of infrastructure projects. This review is carried out by a public agency that is separate from the agency designing, procuring, and implementing the project, or a panel of experts at key points in the project life cycle. The public agency may be the National Treasury, or a special institution created for the purpose. If an independent panel is used, the panel consists of independent experts possessing the range of expertise (typically technical, financial, economic, legal, social, environmental) required to assess projects at each stage. A public agency that oversees the Gateway Process develops the specifics of the process, including maintaining review templates and guidance. The same public agency may undertake the Gateway Reviews, or if a panel is used, the public agency may support the panel's work, including training and accrediting panel experts, and providing support directly or indirectly by facilitating support from other public agencies. At each stage, the public agency or panel assesses the project against relevant criteria for that

---

[18] A. Rajaram et al., eds. 2014. *The Power of Public Investment Management: Transforming Resources into Assets for Growth. Directions in Development.* Washington, DC: World Bank.

stage established in the country's Gateway Process policy. The public agency or panel then provides its assessment of the project's satisfaction of the criteria, including making recommendations as to whether the project should proceed, and any rectifications required to address issues or gaps. The Philippines, for example, has established a Gateway Process for all major capital projects, including infrastructure projects, as well as the activities of SOEs and government financial institutions (Box 2).

Box 2: The Philippines—Gateway Review Process

The Philippines applies a risk-based approach with a single primary Gateway Process, including unsolicited proposals, typically being assessed at the point of submission of the project feasibility study and draft contract. At this Gateway, all major capital projects (MCPs) are reviewed for their fiscal implications—and specific projects are evaluated in detail in relation to the various aspects of project feasibility. The threshold for what constitutes an MCP also differs by context—for example, for national, local projects, national projects, and public–private partnerships (PPPs). Projects also must be resubmitted for approval to the Investment Coordination Committee (ICC) if certain changes occur, particularly increases in total cost above monetary thresholds.

The public body undertaking the Gateway Process and making decisions is the specially created ICC, which comprises senior representatives from across the government. This includes the secretary of finance, as chairman; the National Economic and Development Authority (NEDA) secretary, as co-chair; and the executive secretary, the secretaries of agriculture, trade and industry, budget and management, and the governor of the Central Bank of the Philippines. While the ICC is the decision-making body, the expert analysis supporting decision-making is undertaken by the ICC Technical Board (ICC-TB), which is primarily resourced by NEDA. The ICC-TB also acts as a knowledge hub for line ministries throughout their project preparation, supporting line ministries with direct advice on how proposals can be improved before submission to the ICC. In the context of PPPs, the ICC is required to provide its determination of whether to approve or reject a project within 30 working days from the receipt of a complete set of requirements for evaluation.

Source: Government of the Philippines, National Economic and Development Authority. Investment Coordination Committee, Guidelines and Procedures, 2005; also see in relation to PPPs, the Revised Implementing Rules and Regulations of RA 7718 (The Philippine BOT Law), 2022.

To underscore the importance of the Gateway Process for public infrastructure or PPPs, many countries make the funding required for subsequent stages of the project development process. Project approval is conditional on both passing through the required gateways, and on satisfactorily addressing any recommendations made by the panel during the process. The exact criteria, process, and project tiers vary from jurisdiction to jurisdiction. Nepal, for example, has improved its PIM framework, including implementing a Gateway Process and integrating it with public fiscal management via the budget process (Box 3).[19] The Gateway Process currently occurs within the line ministry that develops the project. Future paths to strengthen the Gateway Process would then involve establishing an independent review function, as noted by the World Bank.[20]

Since all projects are not of the same scale, PIM processes incorporating Gateway Reviews often involve tiered levels of scrutiny, so the resources applied are commensurate with projects' benefits, costs, risks, and special strategic interest to the government. Table 1 provides a framework to summarize the six Gates typically used in countries that have adopted multistage Gateway Processes, including each Gate's purpose and example questions that would be asked at that Gate (footnote 20). These reviews tend to be short and focused.

---

[19]   See World Bank. 2021a. *Fiscal Policy For Sustainable Development: Nepal Public Expenditure Review.*
[20]   This table draws upon content from Department of Treasury and Finance, State Government of Victoria, Australia Gateway Process Overview (accessed 12 July 2022).

Box 3: Nepal—Gateway Process

Nepal has developed a National Project Bank which aims to create a single repository of all projects based on identification, appraisal, selection, and prioritization guidelines developed by the National Planning Commission. For projects to enter the National Project Bank, they must pass through a three-stage Gateway Process:

(i)   Gate 1: The line ministry approves the Project Concept Note.

(ii)   Gate 2: A feasibility study is prepared and must be approved. An additional Detailed Project Report is also required in the case of large-scale infrastructure projects requiring detailed engineering design.

(iii) Gate 3: Projects are selected and prioritized according to criteria outlined in the National Project Bank.

Following projects' approval to enter the National Project Bank, project proposals are presented for approval to the National Planning Commission if they concern capital spending, and the Ministry of Finance if they have recurrent spending implications. These fiscal implications then feed into the budget via budget approval.

Source: World Bank. 2021a. *Fiscal Policy for Sustainable Development: Nepal Public Expenditure Review*.

The Australian State of Victoria's reviews, for example, are typically 5–6 days.[21] From a climate perspective, the Gateway Framework is also consistent with ADB's Principles of Climate Risk Management that focus on both early-stage concept development and implementation. These principles emphasize both climate risk management and climate risk assessment beginning at the concept stage (Gate 1), during preparation (Gate 2), and through to downstream implementation stage (Gate 6).[22] The ability to implement each of these gates is also dependent on the level of institutional capacity and effectiveness of public investment management.

(i)   **Gate 1: Concept and Feasibility**—focuses on increasing the efficiency of government resource utilization by ensuring that, before substantive work is undertaken, the project aligns with wider sector and government strategy; stakeholders support the project (i.e., mitigates the risk that a lack of stakeholder alignment would threaten project success); and conforms to the government's Paris Accords Nationally Determined Contributions and climate policies.

(ii)   **Gate 2: Business Case**—focuses on substantively ensuring that the project is worthwhile to undertake and is a priority. Project merits will have been assessed at a high level as part of investment planning, but at this Gate, the project is at a much greater level of preparation, with the feasibility study prepared—including the likely procurement approach and climate-related analysis of mitigation and adaptation.

(iii) **Gate 3: Readiness for Market**—focuses on ensuring that the allocation of functions and risks between the public and private sectors within the project is efficient and fiscally appropriate, project outputs for climate and disaster risk management are accurately reflected in the requirement specification, and that the project is sufficiently marketable to expect sufficient competition in the tender process to deliver value for money. In addition, with further project preparation undertaken, the business case is retested to ensure the project is still worthwhile to undertake and is a priority.

(iv)   **Gate 4: Tender Decision**—focuses on ensuring that anticipated competitive tension in the procurement process has materialized to generate value for money; that bids demonstrate a project that confirms the business case; that climate disaster and other risks have been allocated between the public

---

[21]   While each Gate review is short and time bound, countries may undertake further assurance activity outside the Gateway Process. For example, the UK requires Assurance of Action Plans to be undertaken to ensure recommendations flowing from the Gateway Process are being effectively implemented.

[22]   P. Watkiss, R. Wilby, and C. A. Rodgers. 2020. Principles of Climate Risk Management for Climate Proofing Projects. *ADB Sustainable Development Working Paper Series*. No. 69. Manila: ADB.

and private sectors along with the costs to manage these risks; and that a robust, unbiased process was used to select a preferred bidder.

(v) **Gate 5: Readiness for Service**—focuses on ensuring that the private operator has complied with all contractual requirements, that the delivery agency has adequate funding to ensure maintenance of the asset in line with climate and sustainability objectives, and that the infrastructure developed substantively matches the promise of the business case and confirming that the project should commence operations.

(vi) **Gate 6: Benefits Realization**—focuses on reviewing whether the project is delivering infrastructure services in line with the business case; if climate change mitigation or adaptation outcomes of the investment are achievable; and therefore, assesses if the project is delivering the social, economic, and environmental benefits it was predicted to deliver.

Table 1: Gateway Process Framework

Gate	Gate Timing	Key Purposes (Non-Exhaustive)[a]	Example Questions (Non-Exhaustive)
Gate 1: Concept and Feasibility	After completing strategic assessment	• Investigate the strategic direction and concept development against agency, portfolio, or whole-of-government goals or needs. • Ensure support for the project by users and key stakeholders. • Confirm the project's initial potential to succeed.	• Is there a clear need for the project? Does it link clearly with wider government objectives? Is there coordination across relevant government entities? Are intergovernmental transfers required for the fiscal sustainability of local government projects? • Who are the stakeholders, and what are their views about the project? • How does the project affect gender or marginalized groups? • Has a preliminary market sounding been conducted? • Is there potential for integration of the project or program with other internal or external government initiatives? • Is the project aligned with Paris Accords Nationally Determined Contributions, and national climate policies and objectives?
Gate 2: Business Case	After concept and feasibility, and completing business case	• Confirm the business case is robust, affordable, and achievable, and has considered appropriate options; the option selected is most likely to maximize value for money. • Ensure the project's greenhouse gas profile is appropriately considered (mitigation) and resilience to climate change's impacts (adaptation). • Ensure that appropriate high-level procurement strategies have been considered. • Ensure the identification of major risks and development of risk management plans .	• Is there a possibility to integrate the project or program with other internal or external government initiatives? • Are assumptions identified and their validity confirmed? • Are the assumptions about procurement and its impact on costs and benefits realistic? • Are there adequate climate-related analyses of mitigation and adaptation impacts of the investment?

continued on next page

Table 1 *continued*

Gate	Gate Timing	Key Purposes (Non-Exhaustive)[a]	Example Questions (Non-Exhaustive)
Gate 3: Readiness for Market	After business case and finalizing the procurement strategy	• Confirm the adequacy of the business case once the project is fully defined and feasibility studies completed. • Review and confirm the appropriateness of the procurement approach, and that it considers the supplier market capability and track record, as determined through a market sounding. • Ensure the implementation plan is detailed and realistic, including the inclusion of a contract management strategy. • Confirm budgetary funds are available for the whole project.	• Have appropriate procurement options been evaluated, including sources of supply? Will the project be sufficiently marketable to generate competition? • Are the project outputs, including for climate and disaster risk management and gender, accurately reflected in the requirement specification? • Is there an adequate probity plan? • Does the contract incorporate adequate governance processes to measure and manage ongoing construction and service delivery performance?
Gate 4: Tender Decision	After preferred contractor selected but prior to contract sign-off	• Confirm the business case when bid information is received and confirmed, and that the contract decision is likely to deliver the specified outcomes on time, within budget, and deliver value for money. • Check the procurement process complies with all requirements. • Check the contract is appropriately drafted to allocate functions and risks.	• Has the proposed solution affected the strategy or expected net benefits? • Have suppliers proposed any alternatives or innovative options beyond a fully compliant bid? If so, how was this assessed? • How have risks, including climate and disaster risk management, been allocated and how will potential scenarios impact the relative cost burden on the government and private operator?
Gate 5: Readiness for Service	Once tender process is completed, and the asset or service is ready for delivery	• Confirm the business case remains valid. • Confirm all necessary commissioning and testing has been undertaken. • Check that all required contractual obligations have been satisfied that arise prior to service delivery. • Ensure reporting and governance processes are in place to manage ongoing service performance and manage change.	• Does the project still meet the business needs and objectives of the government, relevant users, and stakeholders? • Do the assets and/or service meet the contractual requirements? Have any contractual changes been accurately recorded and approved? Has the procuring agency effectively managed and enforced the contract? • Is the delivery agency ready for potential business change? Is it able to implement new services while maintaining existing services? • Does the delivery agency have adequate funding to ensure maintenance of the asset in line with climate and sustainability objectives?

continued on next page

Table 1 *continued*

Gate	Gate Timing	Key Purposes (Non-Exhaustive)[a]	Example Questions (Non-Exhaustive)
Gate 6: Benefits Realization	6–18 months after project completion	• Check whether the service is delivering the required service levels. • Examine whether expected net benefits are being delivered. • Assess ongoing service requirements and confirm that contracts and services are adapting to changes in requirements while not compromising the original delivery strategy.	• What is the variance of service levels to expectation? • Are reporting and continuous improvement mechanisms in place and are they generating results, e.g., root cause analysis? • Are users satisfied with the operational service? • Are ongoing risk management plans up to date? • Does the ex post review audit climate change mitigation or adaptation outcomes of the investment?

[a] All Gates (except the last Gate 6) also involve ensuring that plans and resourcing for successive work phases are affordable, realistic, and achievable.

Source: Modified by Authors based on Department of Treasury and Finance, State Government of Victoria, Australia Gateway Process Overview. https://www.dtf.vic.gov.au/gateway-review-process/gateway-key-decision-points-guidance-and-templates.

Implementation of Gateway Processes: Country Examples

Some countries have adopted complete multistage infrastructure Gateway Processes. Country examples include the United Kingdom, Australia's states, and New Zealand. Others, such as Nepal and the Philippines, have adopted single-Gate processes, while countries such as Bangladesh, Indonesia, and South Africa have created specific Gateway Processes for PPPs.

New South Wales State (Australia)

New South Wales first introduced a Gateway Policy in 2004.[23] There is a wider framework for implementing Gateway Processes throughout the operations of the New South Wales (NSW) government, including defining the gates that can be applied, specifying minimum process requirements, and establishing Gateway Coordination Agencies (GCAs) as the operators of Gateway Processes. Each GCA can then develop its own specific Gateway framework consistent with the GCA Framework, including prescribing detailed requirements, financial thresholds, and other operational aspects. The specific Gateway Process for infrastructure investment is operated by the Infrastructure Investor Assurance Framework GCA.

The Gateway Policy initially only applied to projects over A$10 million. However, following a strategic review in 2013, it was found that using a risk-based approach, which scales scrutiny based on project cost and/or project risk, would be beneficial since a single-cost threshold is an incomplete measure and does not allow for scaling resourcing. There have also been four major updates to the Infrastructure Gateway Process that have seen the process evolve, for example, changes to criteria, scores, and weightings.[24]

---

[23]   New South Wales Treasury. 2017. *NSW Gateway Policy: Policy and Guidelines Paper.*

[24]   See, for example, Infrastructure New South Wales. 2021. *Infrastructure Investor Assurance Framework, March 2021.* The four key updates included the following: (i) Capital performance review in 2013, leading to recognition of the need for stronger investor oversight and assurance; (ii) Auditor general report in 2015, leading to shift away from dollar value toward a greater focus on project risk; (iii) The issuance of a Treasury Circular in 2016, advising all relevant delivery agencies that they were required to adhere to the protocols as outlined in the Infrastructure Investor Assurance Framework policy document administered by Infrastructure NSW; (iv) The addition of Tier 5 (estimated total cost under $10 million) in the NSW Assurance Portal in 2020, to facilitate NSW government commitment reporting, and improved monitoring and reporting of programs and precincts.

There is a panel of accredited expert reviewers from which a review team is selected for a project, and who undertake reviews at each Gate for the project. Panel member performance is regularly reviewed, and membership updated. The tiered approach is designed to ensure the right balance is struck between a robust approach correctly focused on highest risks and achieving value for money. More intense scrutiny is placed on projects that need it most—for example, Tier 1 – High-Profile/High-Risk projects—as represented in Figure 4.

Figure 4: Tiered Approach within New South Wales Gateway Process

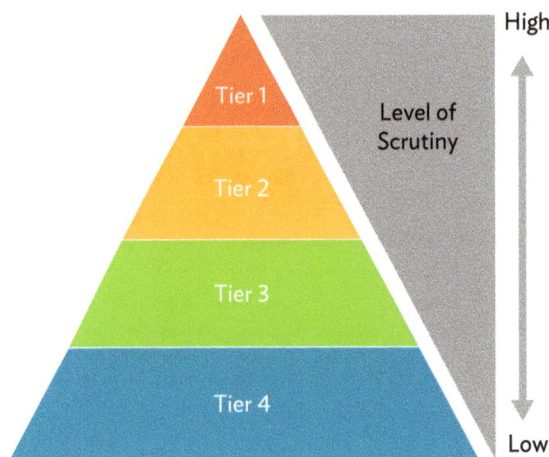

Source: Infrastructure New South Wales. 2021. *Infrastructure Investor Assurance Framework, March 2021.*

Under the risk-based approach, projects are scored based on a qualitative risk profile criteria (government priority, interface complexity, procurement risk, agency capability and capacity). Then, projects are assigned a tier based on their weighted risk score and their total estimated cost. The extent of the Gateway Process that projects are subject to then depends on the project's tier (Table 2). Similar models are used in other Australian states such as Victoria,[25] and in New Zealand.[26]

Infrastructure NSW undertook a review of data analyzed through its Assurance Activities in 2020, identifying the following trends in PIM assurance:

(i)   **Megaprojects magnify risks.** NSW has seen a year-on-year increase of 8% in the value of megaprojects undertaken, with megaprojects now accounting for 64% of total project portfolio value. Although megaprojects possess high impact potential, their size and complexity magnify the range of challenges all infrastructure projects face. As a result, Infrastructure NSW recommended improving risk mitigation and allocation on megaprojects and building greater capability and capacity specialized in megaprojects.

(ii) **Linking investments to community outcomes is a growing challenge.** Infrastructure NSW found that assurance activities identified options analysis and benefits realization as underperforming areas of the PIM process which caused reduced public confidence in project delivery. Infrastructure NSW recommended improving options analysis and consideration of non-infrastructure options, as well as strengthening links across the infrastructure life cycle to bring the community at the center of projects.

---

[25]   State Government of Victoria, Australia, Department of Treasury and Finance. 2019. Gateway Review Process Overview.
[26]   New Zealand Treasury. 2017. Gateway Reviews Overview.

Table 2: Increasing Scrutiny Applying to Higher-Tier Projects in New South Wales

GATEWAY REVIEWS	Tier 1 - HPHR	Tier 2	Tier 3	Tier 4	Tier 5
Gate 0 Go/No Go	Mandatory[a]	Mandatory[a]	Mandatory[a]	Not required	Not required
Gate 1 Strategic Options	Mandatory	Mandatory	Optional		
Gate 2 Business Case	Mandatory	Mandatory	Optional		
Gate 3 Readiness for Market	Mandatory	Optional	Optional		
Gate 4 Tender Evaluation	Mandatory	Optional	Optional		
Gate 5 Readiness for Service	Mandatory	Optional	Optional		
Gate 6 Benefits Realization	Mandatory	Optional	Optional		
HEALTH CHECKS	**Tier 1 - HPHR**	**Tier 2**	**Tier 3**	**Tier 4**	**Tier 5**
Development	Optional	Optional	Optional	Not required	Not required
Procurement	Optional	Optional	Optional		
Delivery	Mandatory[b]	Optional	Optional		
DEEP DIVES	**Tier 1 - HPHR**	**Tier 2**	**Tier 3**	**Tier 4**	**Tier 5**
Any Phase	Optional	Optional	Optional	Not required	Not required

HPHR = High Profile/High Risk.

[a] Gate 0 Reviews are not mandatory when Infrastructure NSW's Risk Review Advisory Group (RRAG) agrees the Review would not add value.

[b] It is recommended that Health Checks for Tier 1 - High Profile/High Risk projects should be mandatory when the delivery phase exceeds 6 months.

Source: Infrastructure New South Wales. 2021. *Infrastructure Investor Assurance Framework, March 2021.*

(iii) **Risk management drives long-term value.** There was a lack of adequate identification and quantification of key project and portfolio risks, as well as risk management plans and risk registers. Improvement and standardization of risk management approaches was recommended.

(iv) **Procuring well is an increasing challenge.** Deficiencies were identified in procurement strategy, including packaging and contracting approaches, clarity of stakeholder accountabilities, project oversight in transitions through the project life cycle, as well as in scoping and cost estimation. Infrastructure NSW recommended reducing market pressures by exploring mechanisms to reduce private operator risk exposure and focusing on how overall project risk can be reduced.

(v) **Governance underpins drivers of success.** Scope for improvement in governance was identified in the appropriateness of team structures and resourcing, and clarity of roles and responsibilities. Infrastructure NSW recommended simplifying and strengthening governance structures and systems, including updating the Infrastructure Investor Assurance Framework, and better information sharing across government to support greater coordination.

South Africa

South Africa's mature PPP program incorporates a Gateway Process with four Gates, operated by the PPP unit established within the National Treasury. The process applies to PPPs undertaken by national, provincial, and municipal government bodies, as well as SOEs. However, exemptions from the Gateway Process do exist in certain situations where more specific regulations apply, such as certain large SOEs like the electricity utility Eskom, and independent power producer PPPs where electricity is provided to Eskom.

The Gateway Process's four stages are set out as follows:[27]

(i)   After the preparation of the project feasibility study (Treasury Approval I), a determination is made to decide if a project is affordable and provides value for money, and whether substantial technical, operational, and financial risk has been transferred to the private operator.

(ii)   After the preparation of procurement documentation (Treasury Approval IIA), to ensure the procurement process is fair, equitable, transparent, competitive, and cost-effective, and protects or advances certain categories of disadvantaged persons.

(iii) After the evaluation of bids but before appointing a preferred bidder (Treasury Approval IIB), to assess how the procurement evaluation criteria have been applied to select the proposed preferred bidder.

(iv)   After procurement but before the PPP contract is signed (Treasury Approval III), to ensure the PPP contract is consistent with Treasury Approval I, and that an appropriate contract management plan exists, and satisfactory due diligence has been undertaken on the proposed private operator. There is also a requirement to re-obtain approval if there are significant changes to a project following approval.

Indonesia

Indonesia's Gateway Process is focused on PPPs, with approval being required by line ministries or other public agencies to obtain a sovereign guarantee for the approval of PPPs. The aims of the Gateway Process are to improve the creditworthiness and quality of PPPs for infrastructure projects in Indonesia. Created in 2009 by the Indonesian Ministry of Finance as an SOE, the Indonesia Infrastructure Guarantee Fund (IIGF) provides guarantees for one single or several financial obligations of a public contracting agency that participates in a PPP consortium. If the economic feasibility of the PPP project is disturbed due to perils caused by the public contracting agency, the IIGF will provide compensation. Covered risks include inability and unwillingness of the public contracting agency to pay due to early termination, or project default due to government action or inaction. This latter category includes changes in law, expropriation, currency inconvertibility and non-transfer, and force majeure affecting the contracting authority. The IIGF typically commissions two separate teams for project appraisal and guarantee appraisal, respectively, to manage potential conflicts between the two.

The IIGF operates as a "single window" to appraise infrastructure PPPs seeking government guarantees and to provide consistency, clarity, and standardized procedures, as well as better management of Ministry of Finance fiscal risk in relation to government guarantees. The "single window" involves the following:

(i)   Improving creditworthiness – bankability of PPP projects.

(ii)   Providing guarantees to well-structured PPPs.

(iii) Improving governance, transparency, and consistency of the guarantee provision process.

(iv)   Ring-fencing the Government of Indonesia's contingent liabilities and minimizing sudden shocks to the State Budget.

---

27   South Africa National Treasury PPP Manual. https://www.gtac.gov.za/resource/gtacs-public-private-partnership-manual (accesses 10 April 2023).

Bangladesh

Like Indonesia, Bangladesh has a form of Gateway Process for PPPs, established since 2015 under the PPP Act.[28] Under the PPP Act, a PPP Authority was created which has roles including appointing advisors, developing and approving PPP contracts, and supervising PPP project progress. The PPP Authority's Board of Governors includes senior cross-government representation, including the Prime Minister (Chairperson), the minister of finance, the minister of planning, and the chief executive officer of the PPP Authority.[29] The PPP Authority currently applies a consistent process across all PPPs.

The Bangladesh PPP process includes independent oversight. Two additional forms of independent oversight exist in Bangladesh for PPP projects. A newly established PPP unit under the Ministry of Finance oversees the fiscal viability of PPP projects and approves government financing for PPPs as well as funding. This includes overseeing the PPP Technical Assistance Fund, Viability Gap Fund, and Bangladesh Infrastructure Finance Fund. The Cabinet Committee on Economic Affairs (CCEA) provides approval at two separate stages (Figure 5): in-principal approval is provided as part of the project screening stage (2); and final approval is provided at post tender stage (5), once a preferred bidder has been selected and negotiations conducted, prior to contract award.

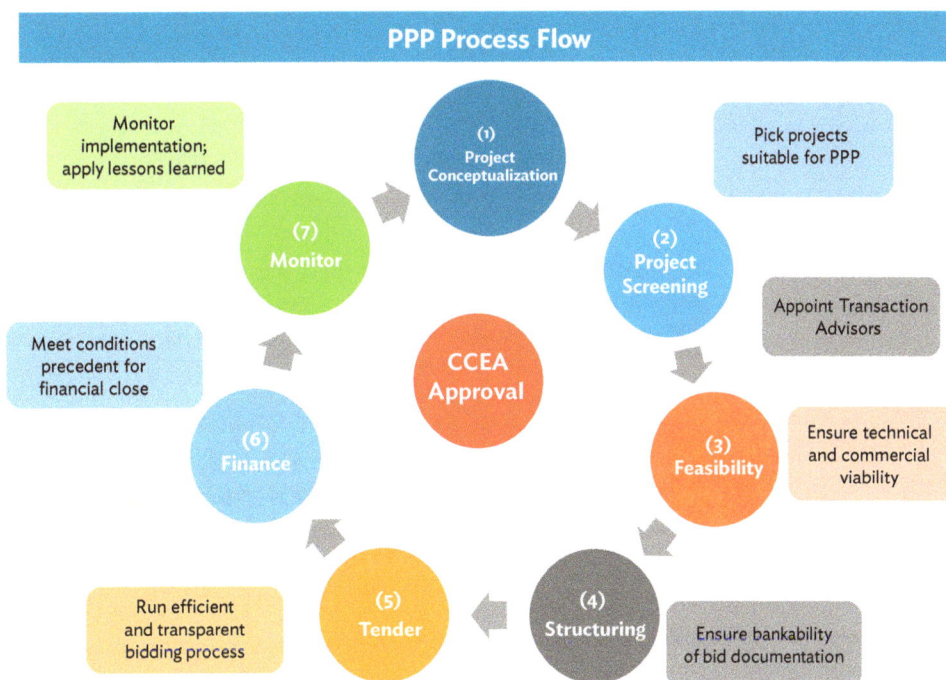

Figure 5: CCEA Approval within the PPP Process in Bangladesh

CCEA = Cabinet Committee on Economic Affairs, PPP = public–private partnership.

Source: *PPPA Presentation on PPP Regulatory Framework*, 2019.

---

28   See, for example, Asian Development Bank (ADB). 2019. Public–Private Partnership Monitor. Second Edition. Manila.
29   Bangladesh PPP Authority, Overview of the PPP Program in Bangladesh, 2019.

4 Lessons for Countries in the Design and Implementation of Gateway Processes

Gateway Processes are a valuable addition to PIM because they strengthen scrutiny at key phases of project preparation with independent expert oversight. In doing so, projects are prepared in a more robust manner, and scarce public resources are focused on preparing the best projects. However, as shown by the country studies in Section 4, the principles of Gateway Processes have been adapted in a range of contexts in different ways. It is therefore up to each DMC to determine how to develop their own Gateway Process within their wider PIM. This section synthesizes key lessons for both designing Gateway Processes (Section 4A) and practical advice on implementing them and change management (Section 4B)—drawing on the key elements and country case studies in Section 3. Like any institutional change, developing a Gateway Process will add resourcing requirements and cost, which must be undertaken mindfully in the context of the challenging fiscal environment countries are operating in (described in Section 2). However, improvements in PIM yield wide-ranging and enduring economic benefits, so it is a worthwhile investment.

A. Designing Gateway Processes

Ultimately, a Gateway Process is an added assurance layer inserted into a wider PIM process. Accordingly, a Gateway Process is only as effective as the PIM it supports—and the institutional capacity possessed across government to prepare and assess projects. This explains why, in places like Bangladesh, Cambodia, and Nepal, Gateway Processes are often added as part of wider PIM reform. More specifically:

(i) **Gateway Processes work best when they act as a peer review process.** Nearly all countries surveyed have either set up separate institutions (like Infrastructure NSW or the IIGF) or approval bodies within existing agencies (like the Philippines' Investment Coordination Committee within the National Economic and Development Authority). Traditionally, such processes have been owned by a Ministry of Finance, but separate institutions can work well by creating organizational focus and clearer accountability and resourcing.

(ii) **A range of resourcing choices are available for the expertise and technical work involved in Gateway Processes.** While the management of Gateway Processes should not be outsourced, the expertise to conduct reviews can be either provided by existing public agencies, or by external experts (e.g., from the private sector as in NSW). While this has a cost, the cost is typically very low compared to the costs and risks of the projects being evaluated. In Australia, the fees for a typical review are $35,000 per review, compared to project values in hundreds of millions, if not billions, of dollars.

(iii) **Gateway Process-operating agencies need sufficient institutional power to perform truly independent reviews.** Nearly all countries have enshrined the Gateway Review process in law. This includes making reviews a legal requirement, declaring contracts as void without the requisite approvals, making successive project preparation funding contingent on obtaining prior approvals, and ensuring senior governmental representation on approval committees. These legal and institutional arrangements support the operating agency to play an effective peer reviewing role. In NSW, the review report is tabled alongside the relevant implementing team documentation (e.g., final business case), when it is considered by the cabinet. Any adverse findings arising from the review would be transparent and obvious to those deciding on the project.

(iv) **All projects involving government funding, regardless of procurement method, present fiscal risk for the government and should be subject to the Gateway Process.** Whether a project is undertaken as a conventional government project, as a PPP, or through an SOE, they all affect the country's infrastructure outcomes and have fiscal implications. While most jurisdictions do not include SOEs in their Gateway Processes, some, such as Australia's states, do. The reason for including SOEs is that they are not only responsible for the delivery of very substantial capital works programs in sectors including water, energy, and transportation, but also that their borrowings are frequently guaranteed by the relevant national government.[30] To ensure that scarce resources are then allocated to their best use, countries have looked to employ risk-based approaches. These can involve both simple monetary value thresholds (e.g., total estimated cost) as well as risk scores (derived from both quantitative and qualitative criteria). Depending on how the risk criteria are specified, it could then be expected that most PPPs and SOE capital investments would be subject to the Gateway Process.

(v) **Countries have designed Gateway Process with varying numbers of Gates, although nearly all at least have a Gate for feasibility study or business case review.** This is because the feasibility study Gate is the point at which the project is assessed as worthwhile to undertake and is a priority. The earlier Gate concerns resource prioritization (avoiding overinvestment in preparing projects that conflict with government strategy), while the later Gates primarily concern whether subsequent project preparation (e.g., receiving tenders) reveals that the business case rationale is still substantively intact. Accordingly, the validity and effectiveness of most Gates depends on the presence of the business case Gate. It is generally recommended that countries have the six Gates as developed by the UK and applied in Australia and New Zealand (Table 2). The key reason for this is the recognition that initial feasibility changes throughout the project life cycle. This can be due to further design development, which provides more reliability about costs and benefits. Similarly, this could be because certain risks are either reduced or increased post procurement, depending on the key contractual terms and conditions negotiated and agreed upon between the implementing agency and the contractor or PPP company delivering the project. Since feasibility may change as the project proceeds through the various stages of development, it is considered appropriate that the approval authority be re-examined.

B. Implementing Gateway Processes and Change Management

Implementing a Gateway Process is a significant institutional change, particularly when it forms part of wider PIM reform. DMCs can best manage this process by obtaining external expertise to assist in the design and implementation of their Gateway Process. Particularly where the process will be new, DMCs can leverage the expertise of both development partners like ADB and outside advisors who have experience in designing and implementing Gateway Processes. If the public agency teams work alongside these experts from the start, effective knowledge transfer can occur, supporting long-term sustainability.

Designing a Gateway Process consistent with the principles of best practice should be tailored to the country context. If wider PIM gaps or areas of improvement exist, it is worth considering addressing these at the same time as the Gateway Process. It can be beneficial to start with a less resource-intensive Gateway Process to ensure the process does not overwhelm institutions. Few countries, for example, use a full six-Gate process. Another lever DMCs have is to adjust the level of risk thresholds. The Gateway Process can then develop and expand over time as institutions grow in confidence with its application.

---

[30]   ADB. 2022. *An Infrastructure Governance Approach to Fiscal Management in State-Owned Enterprises and Public–Private Partnerships.* Manila.

The existing legal and regulatory framework should be surveyed to identify the interactions that a Gateway Process may have with existing processes. In addition, ministries of finance may already have review roles in assessing projects' fiscal implications. These existing processes should be assessed to determine whether they should remain in place as is, evolve, or be incorporated into the Gateway Process. The detail of the process should also be specified in an operational manual to ensure the process can be operationalized—including the documents required for submission at each Gate, and the review time frames.

Like any new assurance process, the Gateway Process will likely have resourcing needs that are additional to the current work undertaken by public agencies. This will require that DMCs develop a resourcing strategy for the Gateway Process and allocate funding to operationalize the process effectively. While this is obvious when creating new institutions, additional resources may also be needed when the Gateway Process is undertaken by an existing institution.

Teams must be trained to build capacity to implement the Gateway Process within the agency owning the process as well as the line ministries that will be submitting projects. DMCs may consider procuring external training support to assist in this. Additionally, the development of standard operating procedures, guidelines, and submission templates help to harmonize processes, clarify expectations, and make the Gateway Process operate more efficiently. The agency owning the Gateway Process can then act as a center of expertise for line ministries, for example, updating guidance as the process evolves and providing ongoing training.

DMCs should create and operationalize a reporting process that generate transparency in how the Gateway Process is functioning as intended. Involved ministries should hold continuous improvement meetings to ensure it evolves as needed. No matter how well the process is designed, as soon as it begins operating, valuable new data will emerge on how the process can operate even more effectively. Institutional arrangements must therefore be established to ensure a transparent reporting process and hold continuous improvement meetings to ensure it evolves as needed. Data for reporting may include the number of projects submitted, the completeness and quality of submissions, variance between actual versus required review time frames, the number of projects approved or rejected, and the categories of reasons for rejection.

C. Risk-Based Approach to Implementing a Gateway Process

There are two key dimensions to the implementation and full adoption of best practice Gateway processes: (i) which projects, and (ii) which Gates. Subjecting all capital projects to Gateway Processes can be daunting and very resource-intensive, especially for DMCs with less institutional capacity and resources. Therefore, countries that apply best practice have put in place a risk-based approach, to ensure that projects that pose the highest likely risk receive the most attention. The riskiness of projects is typically considered across two dimensions—the expected total cost of the project, and a range of qualitative risks, as per those identified in New South Wales outlined in Table 3. A weighted score for the criteria is then compared against the expected total cost to determine a preliminary Project Risk Rating. At the same time, countries that apply best practices for a risk-based approach typically mandate early gates for all projects, regardless of risk rating. While bigger, more complex projects should be submitted for review in the later gates, dealing with readiness for market, tender evaluation, and readiness for service. It is important to note that while all six gates are ultimately important and designed to provide project assurance throughout the project life cycle, the earlier gates are critical for establishing the right footing for a project. DMCs should develop a risk-rating methodology as a priority, to ensure that scarce resources are focused on projects that require the highest level of scrutiny, while also mandating early gates (i.e., gates 1–3), until such time as the capability is in place to extend the process to the full six gates in line with international best practice.

Table 3: New South Wales Qualitative Risk Profile Criteria

Criteria	Definition
Government Priority	The degree of criticality in timing of the project or program due to potential adverse impacts on an existing community or the growth of a new community. The level of project or program priority, where: • the project is mandated through documents such as the NSW Budget, Premier's Priorities, State Infrastructure Strategy. Cabinet endorsed infrastructure plan, Election Commitment, or; • mandated through Ministerial authority or statement that has been made regarding the priority of the project; or; • the project is assigned priority through an agency endorsed strategic document or funded forward capital program; or • the project is assigned priority as an enabler of a mandated project.
Interface Complexity	The extent to which the success of the project or program will depend on the management of complex technical or commercial dependencies with other • agencies, SOCs, nongovernment sector organizations or other third parties—providing approvals, contributing to the funding of the project, or being given operational responsibility, and/or • projects or services where there are fundamental interdependencies that will directly influence the scope and cost of either project.
Procurement Risk	The extent to which a project or program requires, sophisticated, customized or complex procurement methods, therby increasing the need for a careful assessment of the procurement strategy, management of the procurement task, and management of the associated delivery risk.
Agency Capability and Capacity	The extent to which the sponsor agency has clear governnance arrangements, demonstrated capability (experience), and capacity (available skilled resources) or can access these through recruitment or procurement of capability in the development and/or delivery of the type of project or program proposed.

NSW = New South Wales, SOC = state-owned corporation.

Source: Infrastructure New South Wales. 2021. *Infrastructure Investor Assurance Framework—Gateway Coordination Agency Framework for Capital Projects under the NSW Gateway Policy.*

Conclusion

The economic recovery post pandemic has been constrained by new fiscal and macroeconomic challenges. This report outlined the considerable challenges ADB DMCs face, as they recover from the pandemic; confront the impacts of the Russian invasion of Ukraine; and plan for a "green" recovery, involving the need to climate-proof existing infrastructure, invest in technologies and projects that reduce emissions, while also implementing adaptation measures to increase their resilience to reduce economic and social losses associated with climate change. Public investment has the potential not only to raise GDP but also to cause debt-to-GDP ratios to fall, while maximizing the economic and fiscal gains in a fiscally constrained environment. This outcome is not guaranteed, however. Effective PIM and public financial management (PFM) governance is essential to ensure that public investment is of the highest possible quality—that is, the right infrastructure delivering maximum economic benefits at the lowest cost.

The Gateway Process described in this paper is considered an important component of governance reforms required to improve PIM outcomes. But broader PIM and PFM governance reforms are required to secure productive and efficient outcomes from public investments. As noted in a separate ADB technical paper, Value for Money in Public–Private Partnerships: An Infrastructure Governance Approach[31] an effective PPP governance framework assesses and focuses on securing value for money, not at the point of going to market, but at each step in the project cycle. Similarly, effective investment governance is required to manage contingent liabilities and other fiscal risks arising from public investment, and for those arising from PPP arrangements and delivery via SOEs.[32]

Gateway Processes must work alongside broader PIM and/or PFM governance reforms to optimize project outcomes. The Gateway Process is a necessary, but not sufficient, intervention to ensure effective planning and implementation of infrastructure projects. A Gateway Process must also be buttressed by institutional capacity, sufficient resources, and a transparent reporting system to ensure the process performs its intended function to select the best projects and filter out projects that should not be procured and financed. For countries with weaker institutional capacity, this may involve applying the Gateway Processes initially only to the early gates to develop strategic plans in line with whole-of-government goals, and to ensure projects that go forward are affordable, achievable, and likely to achieve value for money. Finally, strong leadership by relevant senior officials who support implementation of the Gateway Process is necessary to reinforce the importance of the work done by the project teams within line ministries and the reviewing agency.

In conclusion, the key messages of this report are as follows:

(i) **Improved project outcomes.** The Gateway Process has the potential to help ensure that infrastructure projects are delivered on time, within budget, and to the required quality standards. A study by the UK National Audit Office found that Gateway Reviews had a positive impact on project success rates, with projects that had undergone Gateway Reviews more likely to be delivered on time and on budget than those that had not. Most countries have designed Gateway Process with varying numbers of Gates,

---

[31] ADB. 2022. *Value for Money in Public–Private Partnerships: An Infrastructure Governance Approach. Manila.*
[32] ADB. 2022. *An Infrastructure Governance Approach to Fiscal Management in State-Owned Enterprises and Public-Private Partnerships.* Manila.

especially in the early stages of the project cycle, but do not have a comprehensive Gateway Review throughout the entire project cycle from concept to implementation.

(ii) **Better decision-making.** By providing a clear framework for decision-making, and reviews by other entities separate from the procuring agency, the Gateway Process helps ensure that decisions are based on objective criteria rather than subjective opinions.

(iii) **Increased transparency.** The Gateway Process provides a transparent framework for project delivery, making it easier for stakeholders to understand the progress of the project and the decisions being made.

(iv) **Overall, the Gateway Process provides a structured approach to infrastructure development that can help ensure project success; reduce fiscal, climate, and other risks; and improve stakeholder engagement and decision-making.** However, the effectiveness of the Gateway Process is likely to depend on a range of factors, including the quality of the reviews, the level of engagement from stakeholders, and the overall institutional environment and effectiveness within an organization. Therefore, while there is some evidence to support the use of the Gateway Process, it is not a panacea, and its effectiveness may vary depending on the specific context in which it is applied.

References

Abiad, A., D. Furceri, and P. Topalova. 2015. The Macroeconomic Effects of Public Investment: Evidence from Advanced Economies. *International Monetary Fund (IMF) Working Paper.*

Asian Development Bank (ADB). 2017. *Climate Change Operational Framework 2017–2030 Enhanced Actions to Low Greenhouse Gas Emission and Climate-Resilient Development.* Manila.

———. 2019. *Public–Private Partnership Monitor. Second Edition.* Manila.

———. 2020a. *Green Finance Strategies for Post-COVID-19 Economic Recovery in Southeast Asia: Green Recoveries for People and Planet.* Manila.

———. 2020b. *Quality Infrastructure and Fiscal Risk – The Importance of Investment Governance.* Manila.

———. 2021. *Supporting Quality Infrastructure in Developing Asia.* Manila.

———. 2022a. *An Infrastructure Governance Approach to Fiscal Management in State-Owned Enterprises and Public–Private Partnerships.* Manila.

———. 2022b. *Asian Development Outlook 2022: Mobilizing Taxes for Development.* Manila.

———. 2022c. *Asian Development Outlook 2022 Supplement: Recovery Faces Diverse Challenges.* Manila.

———. 2022d. *The Sustainability of Asia's Debt: Problems, Policies and Practices.* Manila.

Dabla-Norris, E., J. Daniel, M. Nozaki, C. Alonso, V. Balasundharam, M. Bellon, C. Chen, D. Corvino, and J. Kilpatrick. 2021. Fiscal Policies to Address Climate Change in Asia and the Pacific. *{IMF Departmental Paper}.* No 2021/007. 24 March. IMF.

EM-DAT Centre for Research on the Epidemiology of Disasters. International Disaster Data Base, 2020.

Ferrarini, B., M. M. Giugale, and J. J. Pradelli, eds. 2022. *The Sustainability of Asia's Debt: Problems, Policies and Practices.* Manila: ADB.

Fouad, M., C. Matsumoto, R. Monteiro, I. Rial, and O. A. Sakrak. 2020. Mastering the Risky Business of Public–Private Partnerships. *IMF Departmental Paper.* No. 2021/010. 10 May.

Go, E., S. Hill, M. H. Jaber, Y. Jinjarak, D. Park, and A. Ragos. 2022. Developing Asia's Fiscal Landscape and Challenges. *ADB Economics Working Paper Series.* No. 665. Manila: Asian Development Bank.

Infrastructure New South Wales. 2021. *Infrastructure Investor Assurance Framework.*

International Monetary Fund (IMF). 2015. Making Public Investment More Efficient. *Policy Paper.* 1 May.

————. 2021. Strengthening Infrastructure Governance for Climate-Responsive Public Investment. *Policy Paper.* No. 2021/076.

New Zealand Treasury. 2017. Gateway Reviews Overview.

Rajaram, A., T. M. Le, K. Kaiser, J. Kim, and J. Frank, eds. 2014. *The Power of Public Investment Management: Transforming Resources into Assets for Growth. Directions in Development. Washington, DC: World Bank.*

Rigo, E., C. Richmond, O. A. Olugbade, G. Anderson, M. Atamanchuk, H. Bukhar, I. Ioannou, D. Kale, T. Kass-Hanna, M. Queyranne, W. Shi, and J. Wong. 2021. State-Owned Enterprises in Middle East, North Africa, and Central Asia: Size, Costs, and Challenges. *IMF Departmental Paper.* No. 2021/019.

South Africa National Treasury PPP Manual, https://www.gtac.gov.za/resource/gtacs-public-private-partnership-manual/ (accessed 4 Oct 2023).

State Government of Victoria, Australia, Department of Treasury and Finance. 2019. Gateway Review Process Overview.

UK Infrastructure and Projects Authority. 2019. *Gateway Review Process Review: Report of findings and recommendations.*

Wanna, J., ed. 2007. *Improving Implementation: Organisational Change and Project Management.* Chapter 17. ANU Press.

Watkiss, P., R. Wilby, and C. A. Rodgers. 2020. Principles of Climate Management for Climate Proofing Projects. *ADB Sustainable Development Working Paper Series.* No. 69. Manila: Asian Development Bank.

World Bank. 2021a. *Fiscal Policy For Sustainable Development: Nepal Public Expenditure Review.*

————. 2021b. *Improving the Effectiveness of Public Finance in Cambodia: A Public Expenditure Review.*

www.ingramcontent.com/pod-product-compliance
Lightning Source LLC
Chambersburg PA
CBHW050058220326
41599CB00045B/7456